P9-CIW-119

AMERICAN GOTHIC

THE LIFE OF GRANT WOOD

WORDS BY
SUSAN WOOD

PICTURES BY
ROSS MacDONALD

ABRAMS BOOKS FOR YOUNG READERS, NEW YORK

Library of Congress Cataloging-in-Publication Data
Names: Wood, Susan, 1965– author.
Title: American Gothic: the life of Grant Wood / by Susan Wood.
Description: New York: Abrams Books for Young Readers, 2017. | Includes bibliographical
references and index. | Audience: Ages 5–7.
Identifiers: LCCN 2016044477 | ISBN 9781419725333 (alk. paper)
Subjects: LCSH: Wood, Grant, 1891–1942—Juvenile literature. | Artists—United States—
Biography—Juvenile literature.
Classification: LCC N6537.W66 W66 2017 | DDC 759.13 [B]—dc23
LC record available at https://lccn.loc.gov/2016044477

Text copyright © 2017 Susan Wood
Illustrations copyright © 2017 Ross MacDonald
Book design by Chad W. Beckerman

Printed and bound in China
10 9 8 7 6 5 4 3 2 1

ABRAMS The Art of Books
115 West 18th Street, New York, NY 10011
abramsbooks.com

FOR NAN

Grant Wood loved to draw.

His farming family didn't have a lot of money,
so Grant used charred sticks to sketch on brown
wrapping paper or cardboard torn from cracker
boxes. He drew everything that he saw and loved
around him.

When Grant moved with his family to the city after his father died, his crayon drawing of some oak leaves won third prize in a national art contest. Grant started to take his art seriously. He made drawings for school publications and created scenery for school plays. He studied art lessons in magazines and sold some of his artwork to adults for money to buy more art supplies.

UNITED KINGDOM
LONDON
NETHERLANDS
BELGIUM
GERMANY
PARIS
FRANCE
MADRID
SPAIN
Mediterranean Sea

As Grant grew up, he studied art, taught art, and tried to sell his art wherever he could. But he was frustrated that not many people outside of his community knew about his paintings.

So Grant decided to go to Europe. That's where all the famous painters and painting styles came from, it seemed. They certainly didn't come from the Iowa countryside that Grant loved so much.

In Europe, Grant studied and painted in
different styles. He tried Impressionism. Instead
of painting people and places to look like real
life, the Impressionists created a light-filled
"impression" of reality. Artists, like Claude Monet
from France, used quick, sweeping brushstrokes
and painted unusual subjects like floating water
lilies and frilly ballet dancers.

But Impressionism wasn't in Grant's heart.

Cubist painters, like Pablo Picasso from Spain, wanted to show three-dimensional subjects on a flat canvas. In Cubist paintings, people and places were broken up into a jumble of geometric shapes and shown from many different angles at the same time.

Cubism wasn't in Grant's heart either.

Abstract artists, like Piet Mondrian from Holland, did away with real life altogether. They focused on line, color, and shape in their paintings; they didn't care about making their art look anything like people, places, or things.

Abstract art wasn't in Grant's heart either.

One day Grant walked through a museum in Germany. He marveled at the paintings made by artists five hundred years earlier, during the Gothic period. The faces and places in works by Hans Memling and Jan van Eyck of Belgium were full of painstaking detail, not the hazy wash of the Impressionists. They looked warm and real, so different from the mixed-up Cubist and stark Abstract art. These paintings told a story.

And they spoke to Grant's heart.

Grant decided to go home.

"Stop!" Grant called out.

His friend parked the car. They'd been driving through the Iowa countryside, and Grant had noticed a very odd house.

Like most farmhouses, it was plain—except
for one large arched window on the second floor.
The pointy window was the type found in grand
cathedrals built many centuries ago, in the
Gothic period. Grant had seen those cathedrals
during his travels through Europe.

Such a fancy window on such a simple house intrigued Grant. Who would live in such a house? Especially these days, when money was scarce, jobs were hard to find, and not much at all was very grand.

This window tugged at Grant's heart. Was it possible that artistic inspiration could be found right in his own backyard? Was there a way to combine the painting style he liked best with the people and places he loved most?

His sister, Nan, would pose as the woman in a
new painting. Grant asked Nan to sew a calico
apron trimmed with rickrack, a zigzag fabric trim.
He had her slick down her hair and pull it into a
bun. He borrowed the brooch he'd brought back
from Europe for his mother and had Nan wear it
at her neck.

For the man in the painting, Grant asked his dentist to pose. Grant liked Dr. McKeeby's honest face. From a pile of old clothes that Grant used as paint rags, he pulled out a striped shirt for Dr. McKeeby to wear with some overalls.

Now Grant was ready to paint.

Grant worked long and hard on the painting. For months, he painted Nan at their house during the day. He painted Dr. McKeeby at his dental office during the evening. Grant kept on painting late into the night.

But Grant didn't paint Nan and the dentist exactly the way they looked. He stretched their faces and necks and made them seem serious and sturdy, able to weather anything farm life might throw at them, even a tornado. These were the strong, solid people of his childhood, the friends and relatives he knew as a boy.

These were the people in his heart.

Grant called his painting *American Gothic*.
When *American Gothic* was shown at Chicago's Art Institute in 1930, it caused an immediate sensation. For so long, people had visited museums to see Monet's dreamy landscapes, Picasso's choppy cubes, and Mondrian's bold color blocks.

Now, as America dealt with the Great Depression, those paintings just didn't seem important. What did shimmery colors or strong shapes have to do with most families' daily struggles to keep food on the table and a roof over their heads?

With all of its careful details, Grant's painting looked like real life—and a little more. People saw themselves—and something hopeful, something heroic—in *American Gothic*. Here was a no-nonsense painting of the way things used to be, when honest work and a simple life kept families safe and strong, and even just a little bit grand. Maybe things could be like that again someday. The weathered people in Grant's painting were survivors, just as Depression-era Americans hoped to be.

Encouraged by *American Gothic*'s success, Grant continued to paint the people, places, and stories he knew and loved. Plump hills, egg-shaped trees, neat rows of plow furrows, and ribbons of country roads appeared in landscapes like *Spring Turning*, *Fall Plowing*, and *Stone City, Iowa*.

Farmers and their families planted, harvested, shared meals, and cleaned house in his paintings like *Tree Planting Group*, *Seed Time and Harvest*, *Dinner for Threshers*, and *Spring in Town*. Favorite childhood tales about early American patriots showed up in Grant's *Midnight Ride of Paul Revere* and *Parson Weems' Fable*.

Grant became a famous painter with
a famous painting style—one that didn't
come from Europe. His style was even given
a name, Regionalism, because most of the
things Grant painted came from the same
area, or region, of the country.

But Grant still wore his overalls almost every day, even as he became the most famous artist in America. Because no matter where Grant went, Iowa's rolling plains, rich farmland, and rugged farm folks were always in his heart.

AUTHOR'S NOTE

Grant Wood, born in Iowa in 1891, helped found a style of painting called Regionalism. This movement focused on the people and places of the American Midwest, a landscape of wide-open spaces and hardworking people. Grant and other Regionalist artists—like Thomas Hart Benton of Missouri and John Steuart Curry of Kansas—didn't want to follow European art trends. So they painted what they knew and loved: the American countryside and the folks who lived there. During the Great Depression of the 1930s—an economic collapse that saw people lose their savings, jobs, and homes—many struggling Americans found the Regionalists' clean, clear images of the American heartland and its hardy residents reassuring and inspiring.

Grant Wood's best-known painting is *American Gothic*, completed in 1930 and purchased by the Art Institute of Chicago, where it can still be seen today. It is arguably the most famous of all American paintings. *American Gothic*'s immense success proved that a painter didn't have to live or work in a bustling art center like Paris to become a great artist. Grant showed that even an artist who wore overalls and lived in the Midwest was capable of world-class work. "All the good ideas I've ever had came to me while I was milking a cow," Grant once said.

Grant Wood, *American Gothic*, 1930. Art © Figge Art Museum, successors to the Estate of Nan Wood Graham/Licensed by VAGA, New York, New York.

Over the decades, not everyone has agreed on just who the man and woman are in *American Gothic*. Some have said the man is a farmer, because he's wearing overalls and holding a pitchfork. Others have said he's a small-town businessman, because he's also wearing a formal shirt and suit coat. Some have thought the pair are husband and wife; others—including Grant's sister, Nan—have suggested they are father and daughter. Grant's own con-

Grant Wood in his studio, 1931. John W. Barry, photographer.
Grant Wood collection, 1930-1983. Archives of American Art, Smithsonian Institution.
Art © Figge Art Museum, successors to the Estate of Nan Wood Graham/Licensed by VAGA, New York.

Grant Wood, *Spring in Town*, 1941. Art © Figge Art Museum, successors to the Estate of Nan Wood Graham/Licensed by VAGA, New York, New York.

tradictory comments in interviews helped fuel the controversy, leaving open the possibilities for all of these interpretations.

Some Iowans weren't so pleased with the painting. They thought that Grant was making fun of them. As one woman put it, Nan's face was so stern, so grim, it looked like it could sour milk. Another woman even threatened to bite Grant's ear off!

Grant never meant to insult Midwesterners with the figures depicted in *American Gothic*. "These are types of people I have known all my life," he explained of the painting. "I tried to characterize them truthfully —to make them more like themselves than they were in actual life."

After Grant's death in 1942, the Regionalist art movement declined as Abstract and other styles of art grew in popularity. Yet *American Gothic* continues to fascinate the world. The

image is so well-known that it has been used in magazines, advertising, movies, and even a Broadway musical. Parts of Grant's image are often changed to be humorous—the farm setting is transformed to a beach, for example, or faces of presidents or movie stars are swapped for Dr. McKeeby's and Nan's.

By painting the people and places he loved, by following his heart, Grant Wood changed the way the world—and especially Americans—viewed both art and themselves.

Grant Wood, *Midnight Ride of Paul Revere*, 1931. Art © Figge Art Museum, successors to the Estate of Nan Wood Graham/Licensed by VAGA, New York, New York.

Grant Wood, *Arbor Day*, 1932. Art © Figge Art Museum, successors to the Estate of Nan Wood Graham/Licensed by VAGA, New York, New York.

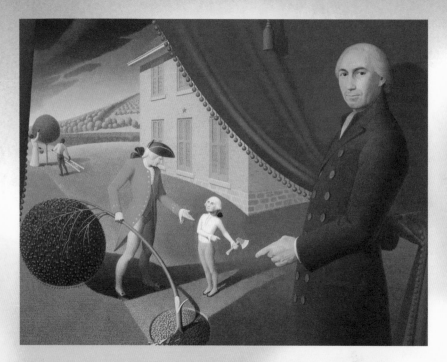

Grant Wood, *Parson Weems'
Fable*, 1939. Art © Figge Art
Museum, successors to the
Estate of Nan Wood Graham/
Licensed by VAGA, New York,
New York.

Nan Wood and Dr. Byron McKeeby with *American Gothic* in 1942. Courtesy of the Figge Art Museum, Davenport, Iowa.
Republished with permission. ©2017 The Gazette, Cedar Rapids, Iowa. Art © Figge Art Museum, successors to the
Estate of Nan Wood Graham/Licensed by VAGA, New York, New York.

SOURCES

Biel, Steven. *American Gothic: A Life of America's Most Famous Painting*. New York: Norton, 2005.

Graham, Nan Wood. *My Brother, Grant Wood*. Iowa City: State Historical Society of Iowa, 1993.

Grant Wood Digital Collection. Figge Art Museum, Davenport, Iowa.

TIME LINE

1891 Grant Wood is born on February 13 at his family's farm near Anamosa, Iowa.

1901 Grant's father dies, and his mother moves the family to Cedar Rapids, Iowa.

1910 Grant graduates from high school and takes summer art classes at the Handicraft Guild in Minneapolis, Minnesota.

1913-16 He takes evening drawing classes at the Art Institute of Chicago in Illinois and opens a jewelry and fine metalwork shop.

1916 He returns to his family's home in Cedar Rapids.

1918-19 Grant serves in the army designing camouflage for artillery.

1919 He teaches art to students in the Cedar Rapids public school system.

1920 Grant travels to Paris for the summer.

1923-24 Grant returns to Paris and takes art classes at the Académie Julian. He travels to Sorrento, Italy, in the winter months.

1926 Grant makes his last trip to Paris.

1927 The artist is asked to create a large stained glass window for the new Veterans Memorial Building in Cedar Rapids.

1928 He travels to Munich, Germany, and views paintings of the Gothic period.

1930 Grant's painting *American Gothic* is exhibited at the Art Institute of Chicago.

1932 He launches Stone City Art Colony and School in the quarry town of Stone City, Iowa, which stays open for two summers.

1934 Grant becomes an associate professor of fine arts at the University of Iowa.

1941 Grant becomes a full professor of fine arts at University of Iowa.

1942 On February 12, Grant Wood dies of liver cancer at age fifty.